Machines Inside Machines

Using Levers

www.raintreepublishers.co.uk
Visit our website to find out more information about **Raintree** books.

To order:
☎ Phone 44 (0) 1865 888112
▤ Send a fax to 44 (0) 1865 314091
▥ Visit the Raintree Bookshop at www.raintreepublishers.co.uk to browse our catalogue and order online.

First published in Great Britain by Raintree,
Halley Court, Jordan Hill, Oxford OX2 8EJ,
part of Harcourt Education.
Raintree is a registered trademark of Harcourt
Education Ltd.

Editorial: Melanie Copland and Kate Buckingham
Design: Michelle Lisseter, Victoria Bevan and
Bridge Creative Services Ltd
Picture Research: Hannah Taylor
Production: Duncan Gilbert
Originated by Repro Multi Warna
Printed and bound in China by South China
Printing Company

ISBN 1 844 43607 1 (hardback)
09 08 07 06 05
10 9 8 7 6 5 4 3 2 1

British Library Cataloguing in Publication Data
Sadler, Wendy
Using Levers. – (Machines Inside Machines)
621.8'11
A full catalogue record for this book is available
from the British Library.

Acknowledgements
The publishers would like to thank the following
for permission to reproduce photographs:
Alamy Images (Comstock Images) p. **14**; Alamy
Images (Joe Sohm) p. **22**; Alamy Images (Michael
Bojang) p. **20**; Alamy Images (Robert Harding
Picture Library) p. **16**; Corbis p. **29**; Corbis (Jim
Cummins Studio Inc) p. **23**; Corbis (John & Lisa
Merrill) p. **5**; Corbis (Pete Saloutos) p. **26**; Getty
Images (NBAE) p. **21**; Harcourt Education Ltd
(Tudor Photography) pp. **4, 6-13, 15, 17, 18, 19,
24, 25, 27.**

Cover photograph of scissors reproduced with
permission of Corbis/ George B. Diebold.

Every effort has been made to contact copyright
holders of any material reproduced in this book.
Any omissions will be rectified
in subsequent printings if notice is given to the
publishers.

The paper used to print this book comes from
sustainable resources.

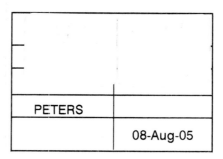

Contents

Any words appearing in the text in bold, **like this,** are explained in the glossary.

Levers can be found all around you. You may even be able to see some from where you are sitting right now! A lever is a **simple machine** that can also be part of many other machines. Simple machines can help us to do lots of different things.

A hammer can be used as a lever to pull a nail out of a piece of wood.

The blades of a windmill are big levers. Wind pushes against the ends of the blades and makes them turn.

Levers everywhere!

A bicycle, a piano, and a windmill all use levers to help them work properly. Without levers, none of these machines would be able to do their job. Even the first computer used more than a thousand levers. Levers are very simple, but very important.

What is a lever?

A lever is a **stiff** bar or stick that moves around a fixed point called a **fulcrum** or **pivot**. Levers are most often used to help us lift heavy **weights**. Using a lever means we do not have to push or pull so hard to move an object. The push or pull that we use is called the **force**.

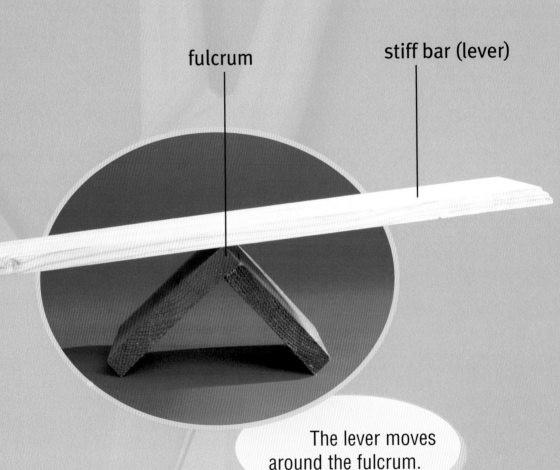

fulcrum

stiff bar (lever)

The lever moves around the fulcrum.

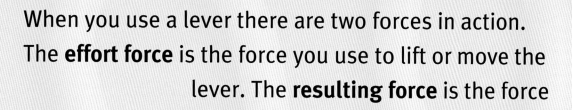

When you use a lever there are two forces in action. The **effort force** is the force you use to lift or move the lever. The **resulting force** is the force that moves or lifts the object. The object you are trying to move or lift is called the **load**.

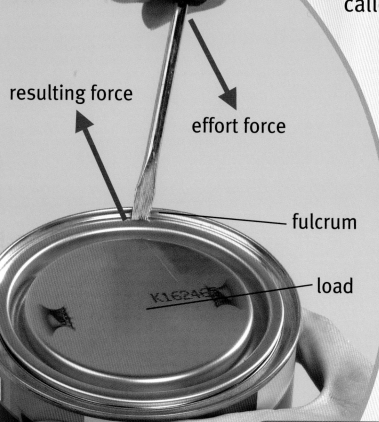

resulting force

effort force

fulcrum

load

K16242

What would happen without...?

Opening this can would be difficult without a lever. You would need to get your fingers under the lid and then pull very hard upwards.

What is a first class lever?

In a first class lever the **fulcrum** is between the **load** and the **effort force**. You push down on one end of the lever. This push is the effort force. At the other end, the lever moves up and lifts the load.

The load is the **weight** of the thing you are trying to lift or move. The load can also be the **force** you need to move something.

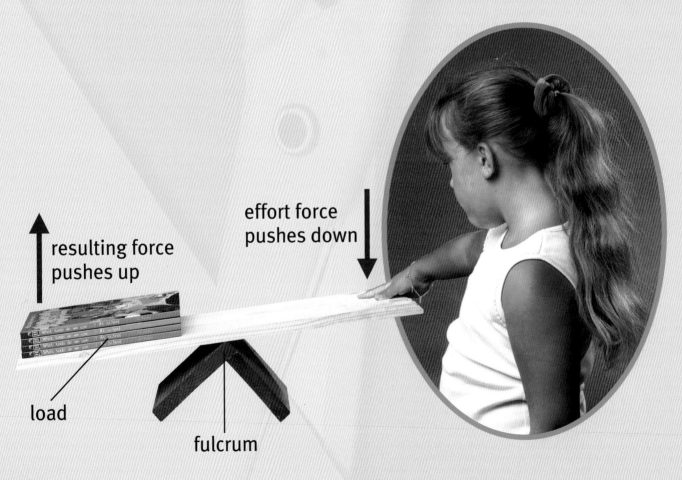

resulting force
pushes up

effort force
pushes down

load

fulcrum

If you move the fulcrum nearer to the load you can lift a weight using much less effort force. The distance you need to move the lever is bigger, but the effort force you need is less.

effort force

resulting force

Moving the fulcrum nearer to the load means you need to push the lever down further, but the load is much easier to lift.

Did you know...?

Anything can be lifted with a lever if it is long enough. If you had a lever that was long enough, you could lift an elephant with just one hand!

Balancing levers

fulcrum

bar (lever)

Scales use levers to weigh things. When the bar is level you know that the weights on each side are the same, and the scales balance.

Not all first class levers are used for lifting things. If the **fulcrum** is in the middle of the lever they can be used to balance things. To balance something, there must be the same **weight** on both sides. With this type of lever the bar is level when the **forces** on each side of the fulcrum are the same.

A set of scales is like a see-saw. Have you tried playing on a see-saw with someone who is the same weight as you? If you both sit still, the see-saw does not move up or down. The bar stays level because you both weigh the same. This means the forces are the same on each end of the lever.

If you play on a see-saw with someone who is heavier than you, it does not balance. This is because the forces are different.

If your friend is about the same weight as you then the see-saw will balance.

The ring pull on a drink can is a first class lever. The **fulcrum** is where the ring pull is joined to the can. The **load** is the metal shape that needs to be pushed down to leave a drinking hole in the can. The lever helps you to open the can without too much **effort force**.

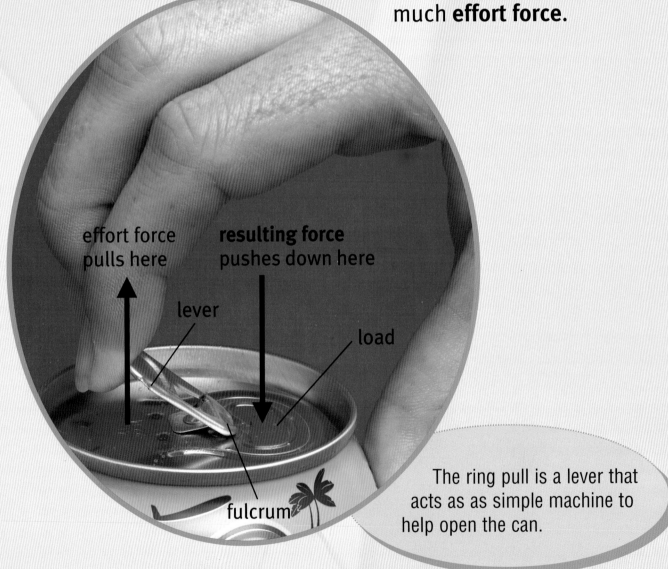

effort force
pulls here

resulting force
pushes down here

lever

load

fulcrum

The ring pull is a lever that acts as as simple machine to help open the can.

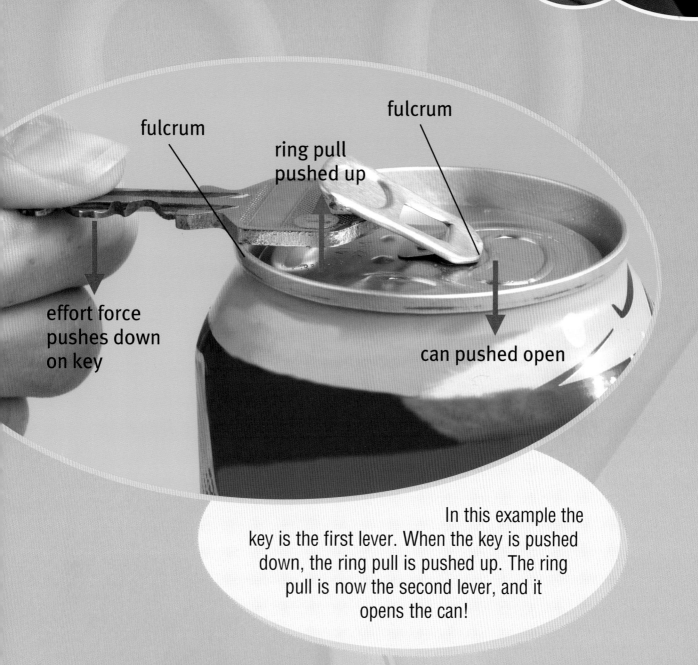

fulcrum

fulcrum

ring pull
pushed up

effort force
pushes down
on key

can pushed open

In this example the
key is the first lever. When the key is pushed
down, the ring pull is pushed up. The ring
pull is now the second lever, and it
opens the can!

You may use a key or a coin to help you lift the ring pull
on a can. This is using two levers together. It means you
use even less effort force to open the can. A machine
that uses two or more **simple machines** together is
called a **compound machine**.

Cutting with levers

When you cut paper with a pair of scissors you are using two first class levers. Each blade of the scissors is a lever. The two levers work together around one **fulcrum**. The fulcrum is where the two blades of the scissors are joined together. The fulcrum is between the **load** and the **effort force,** so these levers are first class levers.

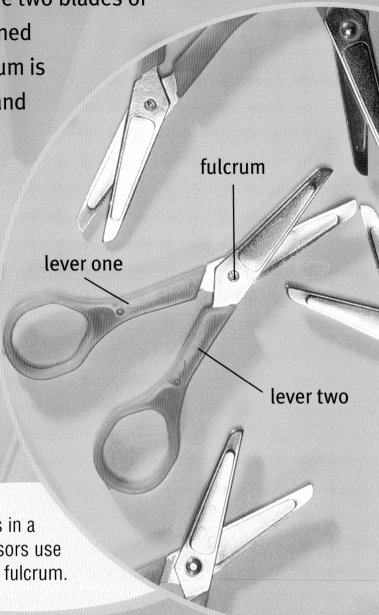

fulcrum

lever one

lever two

Both levers in a pair of scissors use the same fulcrum.

When the handles of scissors are apart, the blades are apart. You put an effort force on the handles by pushing them together. The paper is the load that you need to push through. The blades push against the load. The effort force from both blades together cuts the paper.

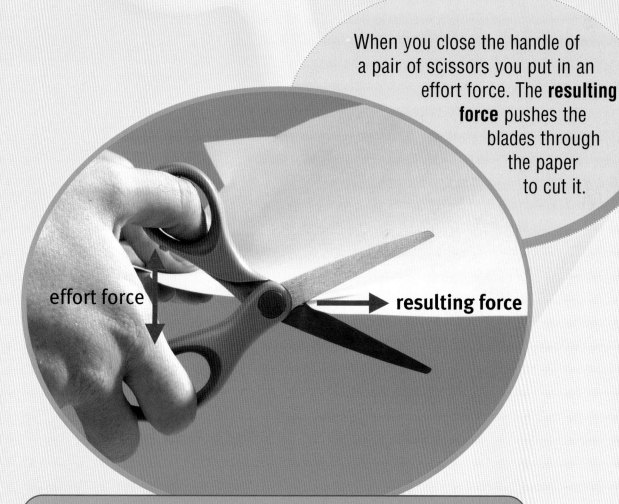

When you close the handle of a pair of scissors you put in an effort force. The **resulting force** pushes the blades through the paper to cut it.

effort force

resulting force

What would happen without...?

Without scissors we would need to use one blade or a knife to cut paper. This could be very dangerous and not very neat!

What is a second class lever?

A second class lever has the **load** between the **fulcrum** and the **effort force**. A wheelbarrow is an example of a second class lever. When you lift the handles of a wheelbarrow you also lift the load. You lift the handles further than you lift the load, but it takes less effort than it would to pick the load up in your hands.

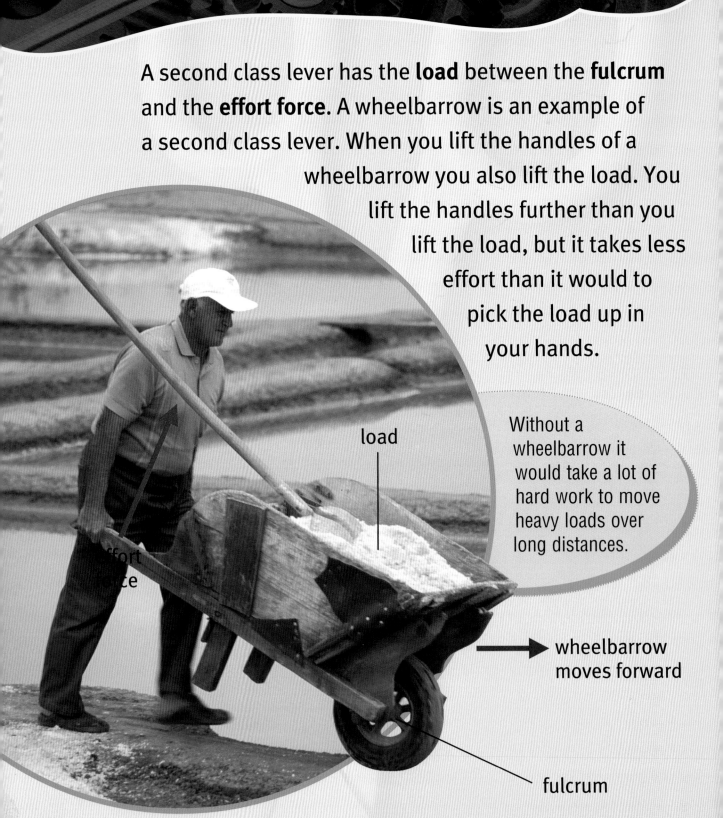

load

Without a wheelbarrow it would take a lot of hard work to move heavy loads over long distances.

effort force

wheelbarrow moves forward

fulcrum

A door is a **compound machine** that uses two second class levers. The fulcrum is where the **hinges** are. The load is the **weight** of the door. You put effort force on the edge of the door when you push or pull it open.

The handle is another second class lever. The fulcrum of this lever is where the handle turns, and the load is the weight of the handle.

fulcrum

handle

effort force

The handle on a door is a second class lever that pulls the door catch in, so the door can open.

Levers in humans!

Your foot is an example of a second class lever. When you stand on tiptoes, the **joint** at the bottom of each toe is the **fulcrum**. Your **weight** is the **load** and this pushes down on the middle of your foot. The **muscles** in your leg give the **effort force** that lifts your heel. When these muscles tighten, your whole body is pulled upwards.

effort force

load

heel

toes

resulting force

fulcrum

When you stand on tiptoes, the load is the weight of your body. Muscles work the lever inside your foot to pull your heel off the ground.

Other joints in your body act like levers, too. In your arms, your elbows work as fulcrums when you lift things up with your hands.

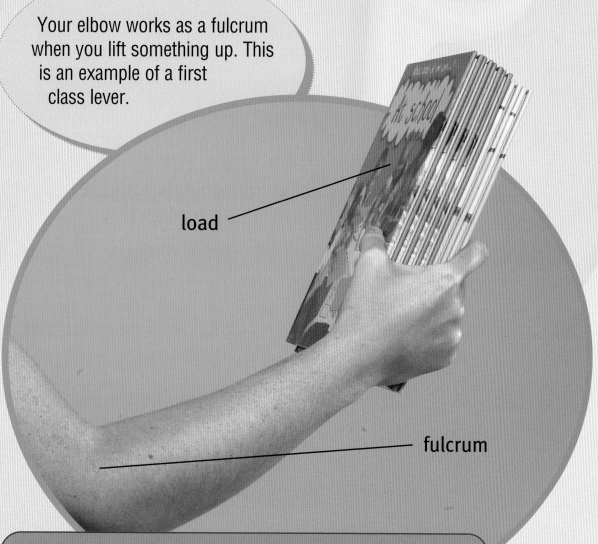

Your elbow works as a fulcrum when you lift something up. This is an example of a first class lever.

load

fulcrum

Activity

You can become a second class lever by standing on your tiptoes. Can you feel your muscles tighten as they work the levers in your body?

What is a third class lever?

In a third class lever, the **fulcrum** is at one end of the lever. The **effort force** is between the fulcrum and the **load**. You use a large effort force over a small distance to move the load a large distance.

The paddle of this canoe is a third class lever. The bar of the paddle is moved a small distance to make the load move a long way.

effort force

fulcrum

A fishing rod is a third class lever. You use your wrist or elbow as the fulcrum. The fish on the end of the rod is the load. You have to put an effort force on the rod with your hand to lift the load up.

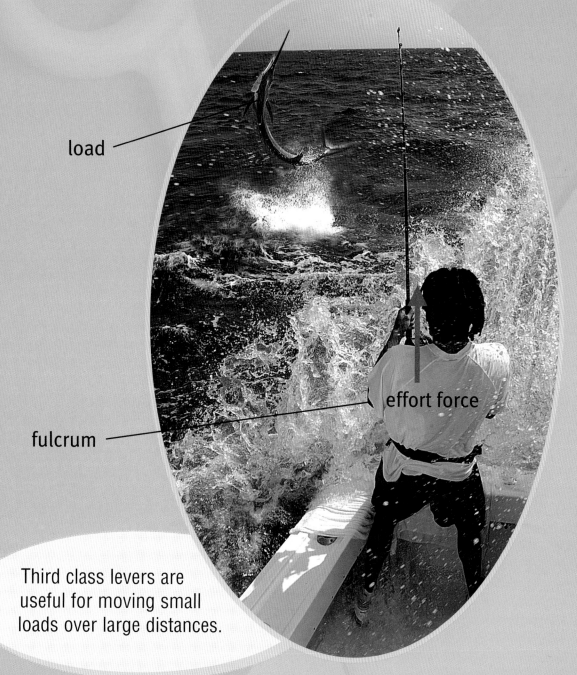

load

effort force

fulcrum

Third class levers are useful for moving small loads over large distances.

Levers in sport

Many sports use third class levers. A baseball bat is a third class lever. It is used to make the ball travel a large distance. The elbow acts as a **fulcrum** and the hands and arms give the **effort force**.

The bat is the **load** you need to move. When the ball hits the bat it moves because the bat is moving. The ball moves from the end of the bat in the same direction as the effort force pushing the bat.

load

effort force

fulcrum

Other sports, for example tennis and cricket, also use third class levers. Can you think of any other sports that use levers?

In tennis the racket is a third class lever that you use to help move the ball over the net.

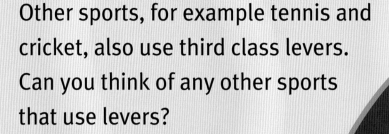

What would happen without...?

If we had to use our hands on their own to hit a tennis ball we would not be able to hit it very far. It would probably hurt quite a lot, too!

Levers in the garden

A spade is a **simple machine** that can be used as two different kinds of lever. When you use your foot as the **fulcrum**, the spade is a first class lever. Your hand pushes down with the **effort force**, a large distance. The other end of the spade moves a small distance in the opposite direction, but with a big **force**.

effort force

fulcrum

resulting force

When you use your spade to lift soil or plants, your body and the spade together become a third class lever. Your elbow now becomes the fulcrum. You use an effort force with your hand at the end of the spade. The load is lifted in the same direction as your hand, but it moves a larger distance.

When you lift soil with a spade your elbow becomes the fulcrum. The effort force comes from your arm as it lifts the soil up.

effort
force

load

fulcrum

Levers working together

A bicycle uses many levers together and lots of other **simple machines,** too. Pedals are second class levers that help your legs turn the wheels. Handlebars are a first class lever where your hands take it in turns to be the **effort force** and the **load**. When you turn right you pull with your right hand and push with your left.

handlebars

pedals

One of the **fulcrums** on a bicycle is in the middle of the handlebars.

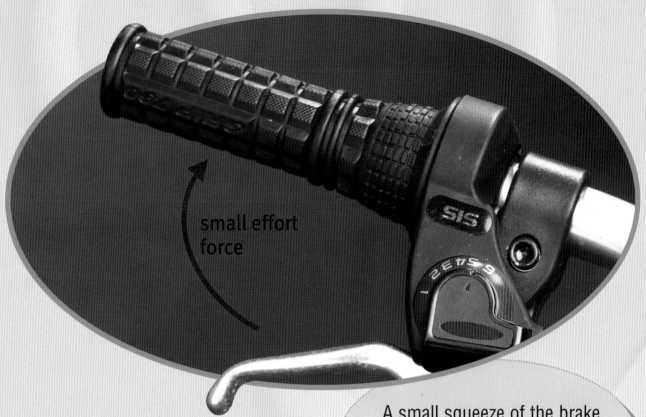

small effort
force

A small squeeze of the brake
lever on a bicycle can stop the
entire load of the bicycle with
you on it!

Brakes are also first class levers.
The small **force** from your hands to
squeeze the brake lever becomes
a big force on the brake cable.

What would happen without…?

Without levers in your brakes you would have to pull on the
brake cable very hard to make your bicycle slow down. This
would hurt your hands and could be very dangerous.

Levers in musical instruments

A piano has hundreds of levers. The piano keys are first class levers that you press down on at one end with your fingers. The other end of the key moves upwards and pushes a second lever inside the piano. A stick attached to this lever pulls the end of another lever. A hammer is then pushed forwards to hit the strings and make a sound.

When you push down on a piano key you trigger a number of levers that are joined to a small hammer. The hammer hits a string which sounds a musical note.

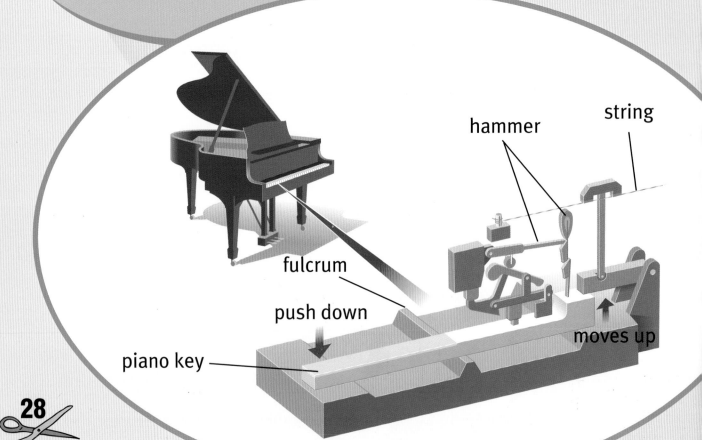

string

hammer

fulcrum

push down

moves up

piano key

The keys on a saxophone are also levers. They are second class levers. The **fulcrum** is where the key joins the saxophone. When you push the keys you move the lever so that it closes a hole in the instrument. The keys also have springs that push the lever back as soon as you let go.

fulcrum

A saxophone uses a lot of **simple machines**.

Find out for yourself

You can find out about **simple machines** by talking to your teacher or parents. Think about the simple machines you use every day – how do you think they work? Your local library will have books and information about this. You will find the answers to many of your questions in this book, but you can also use other books and the Internet.

Books to read

Science Around Us: Pull and Push, Sally Hewitt (Chrysalis Children's Books, 2004)

Very Useful Machines: Levers, Chris Oxlade (Heinemann Library, 2003)

What do Levers do? David Glover (Heinemann Library, 2001)

Using the Internet

Explore the Internet to find out more about levers. Try using a search engine such as www.yahooligans.com or www.internet4kids.com, and type in keywords such as 'lever', **'fulcrum'**, and **'effort force'**.

Glossary

compound machine machine that uses two or more simple machines

effort force force that you put into a lever

force push or pull. Forces can make things move.

fulcrum fixed part of a lever that the bar or stick moves around

hinge piece of metal that holds a door to the wall and lets it swing open and shut

joint something that joins two things together

load weight or object that a lever moves, balances, or pushes through

muscles parts inside the body that help us to move

pivot fixed part of a lever that the bar or stick moves around

resulting force force you get out of a lever

simple machine something that can change the effort force needed to move something, or change the direction it moves in

stiff something that does not bend easily

weight how heavy something is

Index